Interviewing for a Job

by Stuart Schwartz and Craig Conley

Content Consultant:
Robert J. Miller, Ph.D.
Associate Professor
Mankato State University

CAPSTONE
HIGH/LOW BOOKS
an imprint of Capstone Press

C A P S T O N E   P R E S S

151 Good Counsel Drive • Mankato, MN 56001
http://www.capstone-press.com

Library of Congress Cataloging-in-Publication Data
Schwartz, Stuart, 1945-
    Interviewing for a job/by Stuart Schwartz and Craig Conley.
    p. cm. -- (Looking at work)
    Includes bibliographical references and index.
    Summary: Provides advice on preparing resumes, filling out job applications, and
going for interviews.
    ISBN 1-56065-714-6
    1. Employment interviewing--Juvenile literature. [1. Employment interviewing.
2. Job hunting. 3. Vocational guidance.] I. Conley, Craig, 1965-   . II. Title.
III. Series: Schwartz, Stuart, 1945-   Looking at work.
HF5549.5.I6S363 1998
650.14--dc21

                                                      97-51299
                                                          CIP
                                                           AC

Photo credits:
All photos by Dede Smith Photography

Table of Contents

Chapter 1 What Is a Job Interview? 5

Chapter 2 Preparing a Resume 7

Chapter 3 Choosing References 9

Chapter 4 The Job Application 11

Chapter 5 Planning for the Interview 13

Chapter 6 Practice Interviews 15

Chapter 7 What to Bring to an Interview 17

Chapter 8 Appearance 19

Chapter 9 Making a Good Impression 21

Chapter 10 The Interview 23

Chapter 11 After the Interview....................... 25

Chapter 12 Job Interviews and You 27

Words to Know 28

To Learn More 29

Useful Addresses 30

Internet Sites 31

Index 32

Chapter 1

What Is a Job Interview?

A job interview is a meeting between an employer and an applicant. An employer is a person or company that hires and pays workers. An applicant is a person who applies for a job.

One job may draw many skilled applicants. Employers interview the most qualified applicants. Qualified means having knowledge and skills necessary to perform a job. Employers try to hire the best applicants.

Job interviews help employers. For example, restaurants need good cooks. Interviews help restaurant owners understand what the applicants know about cooking.

Job interviews also can help applicants. An applicant might want a job with possibilities for advancement. The applicant can ask about these possibilities in an interview. An applicant can learn whether a job offers the right possibilities.

Applicants can prepare for interviews. They can practice answering and asking questions. Applicants can learn how to have successful interviews.

Employers interview the most qualified applicants.

George Gibson

123 Fourth Street
Villageville, OH 34567
(555) 555-7865
E-mail : ggibson@ohsu.xxx.edu

Education

Bachelor of Arts, Elementary Education   May 1998
University of Michigan, Ann Arbor, Michigan

Work Experience

Jefferson Elementary, student teacher   January -May 1998
- taught unit on personal hygiene
- created hands-on activities for stories

Lake of the Woods Camp
    Senior Counselor   summer 1997
    - Coordinated staff training
    - Supervised other counselors

    Counselor   summers, 1994-1996
    - Supervised children
    - Coordinated group activities

Volunteer Experience

Madison Elementary "Study Buddy" program   1996-1997
- Reading tutor for children after school

Soccer Coach, Ann Arbor Community League   Fall 1996

Activities

- Student president, University of Michigan chapter,
  National Education Association.
- Member of Circle K service group

References available upon request.

Chapter 2

Preparing a Resume

Many job applicants need resumes. A resume is a summary of a person's experience, job skills, and education. Employers learn about applicants from resumes.

Good resumes are no more than two pages long. They are written clearly. Resumes are typed or printed from computers. Resumes should have correct information.

A resume begins with an applicant's name, address, and phone number. The applicant's education comes next. It includes the names of schools. It includes degrees earned and the dates the applicant attended each school.

Then the resume lists work history. It lists the applicant's previous jobs. It includes the dates the applicant worked at each job. It tells the names of past employers. It lists the duties the applicant performed at each job.

Many job applicants also need references. A reference is a person who has worked with an applicant. A reference can tell an employer about an applicant's skills. A reference also can talk about the applicant's work habits.

Good resumes are written clearly.

Chapter 3

Choosing References

Applicants choose references in different ways. They think about their past employers. They may think about people with whom they have worked in the past. Teachers can be good references, too. Applicants should ask each person's permission before listing the person as a reference.

Applicants usually give employers the names and addresses of references. They must give references' phone numbers. People serving as references should know that employers may contact them.

Some employers ask applicants to submit letters of recommendation with their resumes. A letter of recommendation is a letter from a reference. It tells employers why an applicant is a good worker. These letters tell what skills applicants have. Applicants can give copies of these letters to employers.

Employers may ask for letters of recommendation.

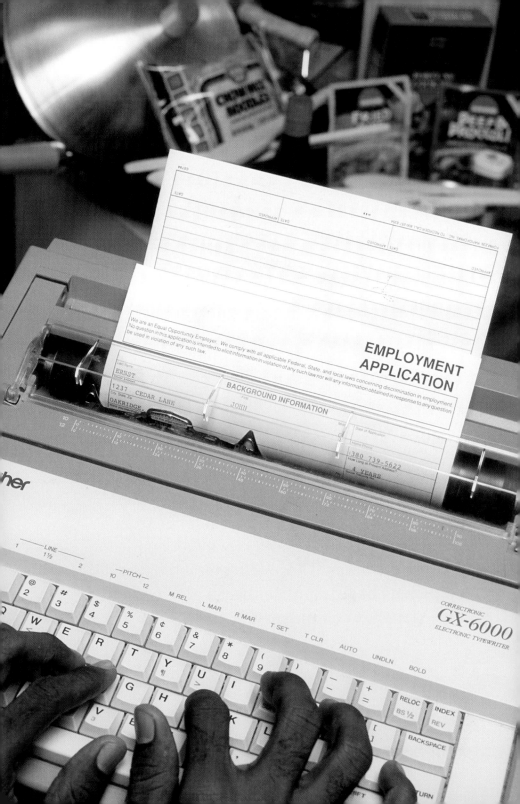

Chapter 4

The Job Application

Many employers ask applicants to fill out job application forms. A job application form gives an employer basic information about an applicant. Sometimes applicants fill out applications at interviews. But applicants usually fill out applications before interviews.

Applicants must fill out applications neatly. They should read directions carefully. Applicants can print with a pen. But it is best to type an application if possible.

Applications ask for social security numbers. Applicants must give addresses and phone numbers. Applications also ask where applicants have worked. They ask where applicants have attended school. They ask applicants to list their skills.

Applications also ask for more specific information. They ask for the addresses and phone numbers of past employers. They ask for the names of references. Applicants should collect this information in advance. Then they have all the information they need for job applications.

Applicants should type job applications if possible.

Chapter 5

Planning for the Interview

Applicants must plan for their interviews. Applicants should plan to arrive on time. They should think about how they will get to the interviews.

Applicants should also think ahead about questions employers may ask during interviews. Employers may ask why applicants want the jobs. They may ask why applicants left their last jobs. Some employers ask about applicants' strengths and weaknesses.

Applicants can prepare answers to these kinds of questions. Applicants must be able to explain their skills and experience. They should know how their skills are right for the jobs.

Many employers ask about applicants' career goals. A career goal is a plan for future work. Applicants should think about how the jobs will help them reach their career goals.

An applicant should plan how to get to an interview.

Chapter 6

Practice Interviews

Many people are nervous before interviews. Practicing can relieve nervousness. Friends and family members can ask the applicant questions about skills and experience. They can pretend to be interviewers. An interviewer is a person who asks applicants questions and answers applicants' questions.

For exemple, an applicant might interview for a job as a child care worker. A friend can ask how the applicant would treat a crying child. The friend can ask the applicant about previous experience with children.

Applicants should practice answering the questions. They should take their time. They should think about what they want to say. When they are ready to answer, they should speak clearly. They should make their answers short but complete. They should give honest answers.

Applicants can also play the part of the interviewer. This will help them understand how applicants look to employers. They will be able to ask questions and listen to the answers.

Applicants should take their time answering questions.

Chapter 7

What to Bring to an Interview

Applicants should bring everything they need to interviews. They should bring several copies of their resumes. They should also bring the names, addresses, and phone numbers of their references.

Applicants should carry their papers in folders or briefcases. They should be able to find what they need quickly.

Applicants should bring pens and note pads to interviews. This is because employers may ask them to fill out forms. Applicants may also want to take notes.

Some employers want to see more than resumes and references. An applicant for a newspaper reporting job should bring writing samples. An artist should bring copies of drawings or paintings. A hair stylist should bring a copy of his or her license. A license is a document giving official permission to do something.

Applicants should bring their resumes to interviews.

Chapter 8

Appearance

Applicants should look their best for interviews. They should wear clothes that are neat and clean. But they should be comfortable, too. An applicant for an office job should wear a suit or a dress. An applicant for a factory position should wear dress pants.

If applicants wear leather shoes, they should polish the shoes. Applicants should not wear hats. They should not wear brightly colored clothes.

Applicants should clean and trim their fingernails. Women should not wear too much makeup. Applicants' hair should be neat and clean. Applicants should not chew gum or smoke at interviews.

Applicants should try on their interview clothing before interviews. They should make sure their clothing is clean and free of wrinkles. This will help applicants feel more relaxed during their interviews.

Applicants should try on their clothing before interviews.

Chapter 9

Making a Good Impression

Making good impressions can help applicants get jobs. A professional attitude makes a good impression. Having a professional attitude means thinking and acting like a serious worker.

Applicants who want to make good impressions go to interviews alone. They arrive on time. People with professional attitudes dress neatly. They bring all the information they need.

Interviewers notice applicants' body language. Body language is the way a person moves his or her body. A person who sits with folded arms looks nervous or angry. A person who does not make eye contact looks shy.

People who sit up straight seem confident. People who make good eye contact seem confident. People who relax their hands look calm.

Applicants should be polite and friendly. They should shake hands with interviewers when they meet. Applicants should thank interviewers at the end of their interviews.

Interviewers notice applicants' body language.

Chapter 10

The Interview

The interviewer will describe the employer and the job. The applicant will learn what the duties are. The interviewer will also ask the applicant questions.

For example, an applicant is applying for a job as a driver. The interviewer might ask about the applicant's driving record. The interviewer might ask about the applicant's knowledge of local roads.

The interviewer will usually ask if the applicant has any questions. The applicant can ask questions about the job. The applicant might ask about working hours. Applicants need to find out if jobs are right for them.

Sometimes more than one person interviews an applicant. An applicant might also meet with a supervisor. A supervisor is a person in charge.

An applicant might meet with a supervisor.

Chapter 11

After the Interview

Applicants should contact interviewers about one week after interviews. This is called following up. Following up shows interviewers that applicants want jobs.

Many applicants write follow-up letters. Follow-up letters should tell interviewers that the meeting was enjoyable. The letters should also thank interviewers. Applicants should write that they are interested in the jobs. The letters should remind the interviewers how the applicants' skills fit the jobs.

Applicants should include their addresses and phone numbers in the letters. This may remind the employers to contact them. The applicants should send the letters one or two days after the interviews. This will show the applicants' interest in the jobs.

Applicants also can call interviewers. Applicants should ask if employers have made any decisions about the jobs. They should thank the interviewers for taking their calls.

Applicants should contact interviewers after interviews.

Chapter 12

Job Interviews and You

Job interviews are challenging. But you can take steps to make them easier.

Prepare your resume before an interview. Put your work history, job skills, and education on the resume. Have your references ready for the interview, too.

Practice interviewing with a friend or family member. This will help you develop good answers to questions that interviewers ask.

Look your best at each interview. Pick out neat, clean clothing. Check your appearance.

Arrive at the interview on time. Be polite and friendly. Think about your body language during the interview. Follow up with a letter or telephone call after each interview.

Remember the purpose of interviews. They are your chance to meet employers. They can be the first step toward finding the job that is right for you.

An interview is a chance to meet an employer.

Words to Know

applicant (AP-luh-kuhnt)—a person who applies for a job

body language (BOD-ee LANG-gwij)—the way a person moves his or her body

employer (em-PLOI-uhr)—a person or company that hires and pays workers

interviewer (IN-tur-vyoo-ur)—the person who interviews a job applicant

job application (JOB ap-luh-KAY-shuhn)—a form that gives an employer basic information about an applicant

professional attitude (pruh-FESH-uh-nuhl AT-i-tood)—thinking and acting like a serious worker

references (REF-uh-renss-uhz)—people who have worked with an applicant in the past

resume (RE-zuh-may)—a written summary of a person's job skills and education

To Learn More

Anema, Durlynn. *Get Hired! Finding Job Opportunitie*s. Hayward, CA: Janus, 1990.

Bloch, Deborah P. *Have a Winning Job Interview*. Lincolnwood, Ill.: NTC Learning Works, 1997.

Marcus, John J. *Complete Job Interview Handbook*. New York: HarperPerennial, 1994.

Useful Addresses

Canada WorkInfoNet
Room 2161, Asticou Training Centre
241 Boulevard Citè des Jeunes
Hull, Quebec K1A 0M7
Canada

Employment and Training Administration
200 Constitution Avenue NW
Room N-4700
Washington, DC 20210

U.S. Department of Labor
Office of Public Affairs
200 Constitution Avenue NW
Room S-1032
Washington, DC 20210

Internet Sites

Interviewing Tips
http://logic.csc.cuhk.edu.hk/~s960467/
   jobprep/interviewtips.html

Planning a Career: A Guided Tour
http://adventuresineducation.org/
   adventur/planning.htm

Successful Interviewing
http://www.dac.neu.edu/coop.careerservices/
   interview.html

The Training Information Source
http://www.training-info.com/

Index

advancement, 5
application, 11

body language, 21, 27

career goal, 13
clothing, 19, 27

education, 7, 27
experience, 7, 13, 15
eye contact, 21

follow-up letter, 25, 27

license, 17

plan, 13, 27
practice interviews, 15
professional attitude, 21

qualified, 7

recommendation, 9
reference, 7, 9, 11, 27
resume, 7, 9, 17, 27

school, 7, 11
supervisor, 23

work habits, 7
work history, 7, 27